Original title:
The Partnership Pact

Copyright © 2024 Swan Charm
All rights reserved.

Author: Daisy Dewi
ISBN HARDBACK: 978-9916-89-229-9
ISBN PAPERBACK: 978-9916-89-230-5
ISBN EBOOK: 978-9916-89-231-2

Crossing Borders Together

We journey on the winding road,
Two hearts united, our shared code.
Through mountains high and rivers wide,
In every step, we seek the tide.

The sun sets low, a golden hue,
Hand in hand, we feel the view.
Voices blend in softest song,
Together here, where we belong.

Stars above in endless dance,
With every chance, we take a stance.
No fence can hold what we have found,
In every moment, love unbound.

From city streets to fields of grain,
We share the joy, we share the pain.
Across the lines, we break the mold,
In stories shared, our dreams unfold.

As seasons change, so do our dreams,
In each other, our spirit gleams.
With open hearts, we brave the test,
Together here, we are our best.

A Story Shared

In whispered tales the night unfolds,
Where dreams and laughter softly mold.
Each secret told, a bond will weave,
In every heart, the love we leave.

With hands entwined we walk the path,
Through stormy skies, we find our laugh.
In silver stars, our hopes ignite,
Together we will face the night.

As chapters turn, new tales arise,
In every tear, in every sigh.
The story shared, an endless thread,
We'll write our dreams in love instead.

Through distant shores, our voices blend,
In unity, we will ascend.
With every page, our spirits soar,
Our story shared, forevermore.

So hold me close, let's write anew,
In every line, I trust in you.
Together we'll craft our timeless tale,
In love's embrace, we shall not fail.

Hearts as One

Two souls aligned within the night,
In every glance, a spark of light.
With every beat, our hearts entwined,
In unity, our fates designed.

Through trials faced and joys embraced,
In whispered vows, our dreams are traced.
Together standing, hand in hand,
In love we trust, on this we stand.

Each moment shared, a treasure grand,
With open hearts, together we'll stand.
In laughter bright, in silence deep,
Our hearts as one, we vow to keep.

As seasons change and time moves on,
In every dusk, a brand new dawn.
Through storms we've weathered, we have grown,
In every heartbeat, we are known.

Forevermore, let's dance this dance,
In every glance, a sweet romance.
With every heartbeat, we're drawn near,
In love's embrace, we shall not fear.

Ribbons of Loyalty

Bound by trust, our spirits thrive,
In every challenge, we survive.
With ribbons tied, our hearts align,
In loyalty's embrace, we shine.

Through darkest nights and brightest days,
In every moment, love displays.
With steadfast hearts, we face the tide,
In loyalty, we will abide.

With whispered vows, our souls are bound,
In every silence, truth is found.
Through thick and thin, we'll hold the line,
With ribbons of loyalty, we'll shine.

In laughter shared and sorrows borne,
In every tear, a hope reborn.
In each embrace, a warmth we keep,
The bond we share runs oh so deep.

Together strong, forever true,
With open hearts, I choose you too.
In every challenge, through each storm,
With ribbons of loyalty, we will warm.

Guiding Each Other Home

In twilight's glow, we seek the way,
With gentle hands, we ask and pray.
In every step, our paths align,
Guiding each other, hearts entwined.

Through winding roads and twisting trails,
In whispers soft, love never fails.
With every choice, our dreams will blend,
Together we'll find the journey's end.

With every wound, we heal in time,
In shared embraces, love will climb.
Through every storm, we'll find our light,
In darkest hours, we'll hold on tight.

In laughter shared, in tears released,\nWith arms outstretched, our fears decreased.
Through every trial, we'll stand as one,
Guiding each other till day is done.

So let us walk this road we share,
With hearts wide open, free from care.
In every moment, love will roam,
Together, dear, we're guiding home.

Hand in Hand We Venture

Through fields of gold we stride,
With hearts that serve as guides.
Together we shall roam,
In search of a new home.

The sun sets low and bright,
Casting shadows in the night.
With hope we brave the dark,
For each has a vital spark.

The mountains loom ahead,
With challenges we dread.
Yet side by side we stand,
In unity, hand in hand.

The rivers may run wild,
But we face them like a child.
With laughter in our eyes,
We'll conquer every surprise.

Each step a story shared,
Every trial has prepared.
With faith our hearts will soar,
Where love will always more.

Weaving Shared Dreams

In twilight's soft embrace,
We weave our dreams in space.
With threads of hope and light,
Creating futures bright.

Each whisper in the night,
Brings forth a guiding light.
Together we will dare,
To make the world more fair.

The tapestry unfolds,
With stories yet untold.
Through laughter and through tears,
Our bond will last for years.

In colors bold and bright,
We paint our shared delight.
With every stroke we find,
A harmony combined.

Together, hand in hand,
We dream, we understand.
With love as our design,
Our spirits intertwine.

Unity's Embrace

In circles wide we stand,
Embraced by love so grand.
With open hearts we share,
The burdens, light as air.

Through storms that bend the trees,
We find a tranquil breeze.
Together we are strong,
In harmony, our song.

With every step we take,
New paths we shall awake.
In trust, our spirits bind,
With every thread aligned.

When shadows fall like night,
In unity, there's light.
Through trials we shall grow,
Together, let it flow.

The world may twist and turn,
But in our hearts, we learn.
In every soul's embrace,
We find our sacred space.

Pathways of Companionship

With open arms we walk,
In silence, hear our talk.
Through valleys lush and green,
Together like a dream.

Each step a dance of grace,
In this enchanted place.
From mountains high we gaze,
The world in endless maze.

In joy we find our way,
Through night and through the day.
With every foot that strays,
We cherish all our days.

Through tangled thorns and blooms,
Our laughter fills the rooms.
In every joy we share,
Companionship is rare.

In twilight's softened glow,
We harvest what we sow.
In love and trust we stand,
Together, hand in hand.

The Sweetness of Synergy

When we unite, new dreams arise,
Together we shine, like brightened skies.
With every shared step, we grow and learn,
In harmony's dance, our passions burn.

Ideas blend like colors in art,
Each voice a note, a vital part.
Through collaboration, we find our song,
In the sweetest of synergies, we belong.

Interwoven Voices

In a tapestry of sound, we hear,
A chorus of thoughts, so crystal clear.
Each thread a story, unique and bold,
Together we weave, both young and old.

Through laughter and tears, our spirits rise,
Interwoven voices, no need for disguise.
In the blend of our hearts, unity sings,
An anthem of hope, the joy it brings.

Embracing Disagreements

In differing views, we find our strength,
Each perspective a tool, measured in length.
Through discussions we grow, expand our minds,
Embracing dissent, the treasure we find.

With open hearts, we navigate strife,
In contrast, we discover the beauty of life.
Through every clash, respect is the key,
In embracing our truths, we learn to be free.

Two Maps, One Journey

Though our paths may differ, the destination's clear,
With two maps in hand, we conquer our fear.
Every twist and turn, a shared delight,
In the journey together, we shine so bright.

We celebrate each mile, the stories we share,
With laughter and wisdom, we venture with flair.
Two souls intertwined, navigating the day,
In the spirit of adventure, we find our way.

Threads of Collaboration

Together we weave our dreams,
In patterns unique and bright.
Each thread a vision, each seam,
Creating a tapestry of light.

We share ideas, breathe and grow,
In the fabric of unity we find.
Strengthen these bonds, let them flow,
With every heartbeat intertwined.

Innovation sparks in the night,
As we gather in shared embrace.
A chorus of voices taking flight,
In every stitch, we find our place.

Through challenges, we stand as one,
Our hearts aligning with purpose clear.
In the sunlight, our work is done,
Threads of collaboration we hold dear.

So let us continue this art,
With each connection sturdy and strong.
In the realm of friendship, we start,
A masterpiece where we all belong.

In Sync We Stand

Together we rise, hearts aligned,
In sync, our goals we share.
With every step, our souls combined,
Facing the world with care.

Through trials, we navigate the maze,
With trust as our guiding star.
In unity's strength, we blaze,
Together, we've come so far.

Voices harmonize like a song,
Echoing through the silent night.
Each note a memory, deep and strong,
In sync, we face the light.

With every challenge, we unfold,
A story of courage we write.
In sync we stand, brave and bold,
Together, we ignite the night.

So let our spirit ever soar,
In unity, we will expand.
In sync, we'll unlock every door,
For in our hearts, we understand.

Unbreakable Ties

In the depths of friendship's glow,
We forge unbreakable ties.
Through storms and calm, we always know,
Our connection never dies.

Every moment woven tight,
In laughter and shared tears.
Standing together, ready to fight,
Overcoming our greatest fears.

Like roots intertwined beneath,
We grow, nurturing each day.
Unbreakable ties, a bond bequeath,
In every word we say.

In shadows cast, we give our light,
Guiding each other, hand in hand.
Unbreakable spirit, shining bright,
In unity, we take our stand.

So let us cherish every thread,
This web of love we create.
In the heart's embrace, always spread,
Unbreakable ties that resonate.

Resonance of Trust

In quiet whispers, trust is born,
A melody soft and true.
Through trials faced, we are reborn,
In the dance of me and you.

With open hearts, we share our fears,
A symphony of souls aligned.
Through laughter, joy, and even tears,
Trust and harmony combined.

Like echoes in an empty hall,
Our voices meld, we sing our song.
With every rise and every fall,
In resonance, we all belong.

Through storms that test our fragile grace,
In trust, we find our way once more.
Together, forging sacred space,
In unity, our spirits soar.

So let the chords of trust resound,
In every heartbeat, clear and bright.
With every step, we're tightly bound,
In resonance, we spread our light.

Unity's Anthem

In the heart where we stand strong,
Voices blend, a perfect song.
Together we rise, never apart,
Harmony lives in each heart.

Hands joined, we build our fate,
With every step, we elevate.
Diverse paths woven tight,
In unity, we find our light.

Mountains moved by our embrace,
In every soul, a sacred space.
Shadows fade as we unite,
Together, we shine bright.

Through storms and trials, we march on,
With courage, we greet the dawn.
For in the strength of many,
A force unstoppable, uncanny.

With love as our guiding star,
No distance can keep us far.
In every heartbeat, we belong,
Together, we're forever strong.

Emblazoned in Existence

Life's canvas brushed with dreams,
Each stroke bright, or so it seems.
Colors mingling, hearts collide,
In existence, we confide.

From silence, we find our voice,
In unity, we make our choice.
Emblazoned bright across the skies,
Our spirits soar, we rise.

Moments shared, a silent pact,
In our hearts, a true fact.
Boundless joy, a cherished glance,
In existence, we find our dance.

Together we craft our fate,
With love, we resonate.
In every heartbeat, we create,
An artwork that won't abate.

Eternally blazing, a sacred fire,
In unity, we aspire.
Let our legacy be known,
In existence, we have grown.

Bonded by Dreams

In the twilight's gentle grace,
We find our dreams, our sacred space.
Whispers echo through the night,
Bonded by hopes, we take flight.

Through every challenge we embrace,
Together, we find our place.
In the tapestry of time,
Dreams unite, pure and sublime.

Each heartbeat a silent vow,
In the present, here and now.
With every vision, we ignite,
Together, we shine so bright.

With courage, we face the unknown,
In unity, we have grown.
Our strengths merge, a powerful stream,
Forever bonded by dreams.

Let the stars be our guide,
In this journey, side by side.
With love, we'll write our fate,
In dreams, we elevate.

Unity in Motion

In the pulse of every street,
We gather, hearts in beat.
Hands together, spirits soar,
Unity in motion, evermore.

Every step a shared delight,
Together we chase the light.
In the rhythm of our stride,
Side by side, we will abide.

Through the dance of life, we weave,
In each other, we believe.
Boundless energy flows free,
Unity in motion, we will be.

Voices join in sweet refrain,
Singing joy, conquering pain.
For in togetherness, we find,
A love that's truly blind.

Carving paths with every dream,
Unified, our spirits beam.
In every heartbeat, a connection,
Unity in motion, pure perfection.

Across the Horizon We Meet

In the dawn's gentle light, we rise,
A landscape stretching wide and free.
With whispered dreams that touch the skies,
Together, we will always be.

Across the horizon, hopes ignite,
A promise held within the sun.
Each step we take, a shared delight,
Our souls as one, we've just begun.

In shadows cast by twilight's glow,
We find the strength to face the night.
With every wave, a river flows,
Together, we embrace the fight.

Each moment spent, a thread we weave,
The tapestry of dreams we've sown.
In every tale, we dare believe,
Across the horizon, love has grown.

As stars align in velvet skies,
Our spirits soar, forever free.
With open hearts, we'll always rise,
In unity, just you and me.

Shared Footprints in Time

In the sands of time we stroll,
With footprints marking where we've been.
Each grain a story, heart, and soul,
Together, writing life's great scene.

Through laughter shared and tears we shed,
Our paths entwined like vines that climb.
In every word that's left unsaid,
We craft the essence of our rhyme.

With every step, a memory born,
A journey shared through thick and thin.
Through golden days and nights that mourn,
In every loss, we find a win.

The sunset paints the sky so bright,
Reflecting all the love we've found.
In melodies of day and night,
Our heartbeat makes a sacred sound.

As seasons pass and years unfold,
With every moment, trust we build.
In echoes of the tales retold,
Shared footprints in time, love fulfilled.

The Pulse of Partnership

In moments soft, we share our dreams,
The pulse of us, a steady beat.
Through life's great maze, we're not just seams,
Together, we complete the feat.

With hands entwined, we walk the line,
Our laughter dances through the air.
In whispered hopes, our spirits shine,
A bond that grows beyond compare.

Each challenge faced becomes our muse,
In trials, strength and grace we find.
Through every joy, we both refuse,
To leave each other far behind.

With every glance, a secret shared,
A language only we can know.
Together, fiercely we have dared,
To plant the seeds and watch them grow.

As time unfolds, we'll brave the storms,
With love's embrace to guide our way.
In every heartbeat, warmth transforms,
The pulse of partnership holds sway.

Intertwined Fates

In the dance of stars above,
Our fates entwined like ivy grow.
In silent whispers, hearts speak love,
Together, through the ebb and flow.

Through all the trials, we prevail,
With hands that clasp, we rise anew.
In every breath, we leave a trail,
A journey mapped for me and you.

The tapestry of life we weave,
With colors bright and shadows deep.
In every moment, we believe,
Our intertwined fates, one to keep.

As seasons turn and rivers flow,
We'll paint our dreams on time's vast face.
In each embrace, our spirits glow,
Together, we have found our place.

When twilight falls and stars ignite,
With every glance, our souls entwine.
In love's great dance, we claim the night,
Intertwined fates, forever shine.

Bonds Beyond Words

In silence, hearts connect and weave,
Threads of trust that none can cleave.
A glance, a sigh, a knowing smile,
In every moment, love's sweet style.

When laughter dances in the air,
Unspoken joy, a bond so rare.
Through trials faced, side by side,
Together, we take every stride.

The warmth of hands, a gentle touch,
In our embrace, we find so much.
Words may falter, but love remains,
In whispered dreams and soft refrains.

Within our gaze, a depth profound,
In understanding, we are bound.
Through seasons change, our spirits soar,
In every silence, we love more.

Together still, through dark and light,
Our bond transcends the endless night.
In the space where words can't go,
A tapestry of love we sow.

Echoes of Alliance

Two voices blend, a harmony,
In each note, a shared decree.
Together we rise, facing the storm,
In unity, our hearts stay warm.

Through every challenge, we stand tall,
In our connection, we will not fall.
The whispers of trust guide the way,
In the echoes of us, brighter days.

Side by side, we chase the dreams,
Hand in hand, we're stronger, it seems.
Every path we take entwines,
In the dance of fate, our love shines.

In laughter shared, our spirits sing,
Together, we face whatever life brings.
With every heartbeat, we create,
A legacy that will never abate.

In the quiet moments, we reflect,
On the bonds we chose to protect.
The strength of us, a sacred pact,
In echoes of alliance, love intact.

Navigating Life Together

Along the shores of changing tides,
We find our way, with hearts as guides.
Every turn brings new terrain,
Through laughter, joy, and some pain.

With compass set to trust and care,
In every journey, we are a pair.
Mountains tall and valleys deep,
Together, promises we keep.

In shadows cast, we share the light,
As partners in this endless flight.
The map is drawn by love so true,
With every step, I walk with you.

Through storms we weather, side by side,
In every storm, our hearts abide.
Navigating dreams with open hearts,
In unity, our journey starts.

As years go by and seasons change,
We're forever bound, never estranged.
In life's great ocean, we will find,
A treasure trove of love combined.

The Art of Companionship

In gentle strokes, we paint our days,
With colors bright, in myriad ways.
Each moment cherished, brush applied,
In the canvas of life, we abide.

Through laughter's hues and shadows cast,
Our bond, a masterpiece so vast.
With every trial, we find our way,
Transforming nights into bright days.

In the gallery of shared delight,
We celebrate love's purest light.
Each memory, a work of art,
In total harmony, heart to heart.

With open minds and hands so free,
We sculpt our dreams in unity.
The art of sharing, a tender grace,
In every touch, we find our place.

Together we create, explore,
The joys of life we can't ignore.
In the realm of love, we engage,
The art of companionship, our stage.

Lines of Loyalty

In silence we stand, side by side,
Through darkened paths, our hearts collide.
In storms we weather, trust won't stray,
Bound by loyalty, come what may.

With whispered vows, we rise anew,
Through trials faced, our bond we strew.
In laughter shared, and tears that flow,
Together we thrive, together we grow.

The Heartbeat of Us

In every pulse, a story lives,
Tales of laughter, of love it gives.
The rhythm flows, steady and true,
A heart composed, just me and you.

With every beat, we find our way,
In moments cherished, night and day.
No distance great, no time to part,
For you, my love, are my very heart.

In the Spirit of Companionship

Together we walk, through thick and thin,
Hand in hand, where dreams begin.
In each shared glance, a bond so rare,
In the spirit of friendship, we lay bare.

With open arms, through storms we tread,
In every challenge, with hearts we wed.
For moments shared, and laughter bright,
In the spirit of companionship, we ignite.

Between Fates We Stand

In the shadow of fate, our paths aligned,
Through whispered winds, our hearts designed.
With courage found, we face the night,
Between fates we stand, holding tight.

With every step, uncertainties loom,
Yet in your presence, I find my room.
Through twists and turns, love's guiding hand,
Together we journey, between fates we stand.

The Dance of Allies

In the twilight's embrace we stand,
Hands entwined across the land.
With hearts aligned, we spin and sway,
Together we'll find our way.

When shadows fall and doubts arise,
We'll light the path, break through the skies.
In unity, our spirits soar,
A dance of strength, forever more.

Each step we take, a story told,
With every movement, we grow bold.
Through trials faced, our bonds ignite,
A beacon shining in the night.

With laughter shared and tears embraced,
We navigate time, our fears displaced.
Together we're more, we rise and cheer,
In this great dance, we lose all fear.

So raise your voice, let it resound,
In every heart, a purpose found.
The rhythm carries us along,
Together, allies, forever strong.

In Sync with Tomorrow

The dawn will break with dreams in tow,
In sync, we rise, let visions flow.
With every heartbeat, time unfolds,
Together, crafting futures bold.

We walk as one on paths anew,
Bright potential in all we do.
With hope as our guide, we will explore,
Embracing change, we seek for more.

Through every challenge, hand in hand,
We build a bridge across the land.
The tapestry of life we weave,
In unison, we dare believe.

With whispers soft, we sow the seeds,
Of strength and courage, love, and deeds.
As seasons shift and moments blend,
In sync with tomorrow, we will mend.

In dreams we trust, with hearts so bright,
Together shining in the night.
With purpose clear and spirits high,
For in our bond, we will not die.

Two Hearts, One Path

Two hearts converge on a winding road,
With rhythms matched, a shared abode.
In every pulse, a promise true,
Together we blaze, there's nothing we can't do.

Through sunlit days and storms of night,
We navigate with pure delight.
In laughter shared and silence deep,
In each moment, a bond we keep.

With trust as our shield, we face the trials,
In unity forged, we walk for miles.
With every step, a story we write,
Two hearts in sync, embracing the light.

Challenges rise like waves at sea,
Yet side by side, we're always free.
With strength drawn from love's warm embrace,
Together, we dance in time and space.

As seasons shift and time unfolds,
Our journey rich, our love behold.
For two hearts, one path is a way to thrive,
In each other's warmth, we come alive.

Whispers of Collaboration

In the quiet moments, ideas bloom,
Together we gather, dispelling gloom.
With open ears and hearts so pure,
Whispers of hope, our thoughts ensure.

With every exchange, a spark ignites,
In collaborative hues, our future lights.
Ideas intertwine, a beautiful dance,
In the realm of dreams, we take our chance.

Through dialogue rich, we unearth the gold,
In unity's arms, our visions unfold.
With minds aligned, we'll craft anew,
The world transformed by me and you.

In every voice, a treasure lies,
Collective wisdom, helping us rise.
Our hands together, we build and create,
Whispers of collaboration, shaping our fate.

So let us share the burdens we bear,
In every heartbeat, we'll show we care.
Together we'll rise, daring to strive,
In whispers and dreams, we come alive.

Threads of Togetherness

In the loom of life, we weave
Colors bright, a shared reprieve.
Hand in hand, we'll face the night,
With every thread, we hold on tight.

Every laugh, a stitch so neat,
In every challenge, hearts will meet.
From the fabric of our dreams,
We craft a bond, or so it seems.

In gentle moments, we create,
A tapestry that won't abate.
With whispers soft, we'll find our way,
Through every dawn and fading day.

Each story shared, a nuanced hue,
In unity, we're brave and true.
Together forged, we're strong and free,
Threads of togetherness, you and me.

As seasons change, our colors blend,
A legacy that will not end.
For in this weave, we're intertwined,
A vibrant life, beautifully designed.

Harmony in Divergence

In varying paths, we find our song,
Different notes, yet we belong.
Like rivers flowing side by side,
In vibrant harmony, we abide.

Embrace the change; it's not a fear,
In differing views, the truth is near.
With open hearts, we share the light,
In every shade, we shine so bright.

The dance of life, a careful sway,
Our myriad steps create the way.
Like stars that shine in different skies,
Together bright, we harmonize.

In every discord, a chance to learn,
For in divergence, our souls discern.
Each twist and turn, a tale to find,
In harmony, we're intertwined.

So let us sing our unique tune,
From morning light to the silver moon.
In every difference, love's embrace,
In harmony, we find our place.

Echoes of Trust

Whispers in the quiet night,
Moments shared, hearts taking flight.
In every glance, a promise made,
Echoes of trust that won't soon fade.

Through trials faced, we stand our ground,
In silent vows, our strength is found.
With every word, a bond we cast,
In echoes of trust, our shadows last.

As storms may rage and shadows creep,
In each other, our secrets keep.
With open arms, we face the storm,
In trusting hearts, we find our form.

The path is long, and yet we're bold,
In stories shared, our souls unfold.
Through every fear, we find a way,
Echoes of trust guide us each day.

With every step, we pave the track,
Together, there's no looking back.
In this dance, our hearts align,
Echoes of trust, forever entwined.

Synergy of Souls

In every glance, a spark ignites,
Two souls entwined, reaching new heights.
With every gesture, love unfolds,
A synergy of souls, pure and bold.

Together we rise, no longer alone,
Building bridges, making new homes.
In laughter shared, our spirits soar,
In this dance of life, we seek for more.

With every dream, a shared embrace,
In each heartbeat, we find our place.
As two become one in cosmic light,
A synergy of souls, forever bright.

In whispers soft, secrets unfold,
Together we fashion a story told.
Through trials faced and victories won,
In unity, our lives are spun.

With every dawn, a chance to grow,
In the tapestry of life, we glow.
Together we weave, a tale anew,
Synergy of souls, ever true.

The Bridge Between Us

In twilight's glow, we stand apart,
A bridge of dreams connects our hearts.
Through whispered winds, our hopes take flight,
Two souls entwined, embracing the night.

Each step we take, a story unfolds,
In laughter shared, our love beholds.
Across the chasm, we reach with grace,
In this sacred space, we find our place.

The river flows, a gentle stream,
Carving paths as we dare to dream.
Hand in hand, we close the gap,
In every moment, we bridge the map.

Through storms and trials, we still prevail,
The bond we share, a timeless tale.
Together we rise, unbroken trust,
Forever we'll shine, a bridge of us.

In every heartbeat, a promise made,
A legacy of love that won't fade.
With every breath, we nurture the flame,
In this bridge between us, love's the name.

Weaving Our Futures

Threads of gold in twilight's weave,
Each moment stitched, a dream to believe.
With careful hands, we craft the day,
A tapestry bright, unfolding our way.

In colors bold, our hopes align,
Together we rise, in day and in shine.
With every knot, the past we embrace,
Weaving our futures, a sacred space.

Through trials faced, the fabric shows,
Strength in the seams, as our love grows.
In patterns rich, our paths intertwine,
Creating a life, both yours and mine.

With joy and laughter, we draw the thread,
In moments we cherish, our journey is spread.
Together we dream, forever we stand,
In the weave of our futures, hand in hand.

As the loom spins on, our story unfolds,
A vibrant narrative, in colors bold.
In every stitch, our spirit ignites,
Weaving our futures, two hearts take flight.

Embracing the Unseen

In shadows deep, where silence dwells,
We find the truth that softly tells.
A glance beyond the visible sphere,
Embracing whispers only we hear.

The moonlight dances on whispers of night,
Holding our dreams, just out of sight.
In every heartbeat, a secret shared,
Through unseen paths, our spirits bared.

We tread the edges of fate, entwined,
In the depths of darkness, our souls aligned.
With every breath, we challenge the veil,
In embracing the unseen, we shall prevail.

Through moments fleeting, we gather the light,
In the quiet, we find our flight.
With courage bold, we rise and soar,
Embracing the unseen, forevermore.

In the chamber of hearts, where dreamers dwell,
We weave the tales we know so well.
Together we shine, in shadows we glean,
In the embrace of the unseen, we are seen.

Fusion of Visions

In the realm where dreams collide,
Two visions dance, side by side.
A spark ignites, a vivid hue,
In this fusion, I find you.

With every thought, new worlds arise,
In the tapestry of endless skies.
Together we build, brick by brick,
Creating a future, vibrant and quick.

Hand in hand, we chase the dawn,
In the harmony, we're never forlorn.
A melody sweet, our hearts compose,
In this fusion, love always grows.

Through storms we weather, side by side,
With open hearts, in truth we abide.
In every glance, a promise to keep,
A fusion of visions, dreams run deep.

With passion's fire, our spirits ignite,
In this canvas, we find our light.
Together we'll soar, in unity's guise,
In the fusion of visions, our love never dies.

Twilight of Independence

In the quiet dusk we stand,
Shadows stretch across the land.
Freedom's glow begins to fade,
Promises made, now just a shade.

Whispers haunt the falling night,
As stars awaken, shining bright.
Choices linger in the breeze,
Like leaves dancing from the trees.

The echoes of what once was strong,
Linger in the heart's sweet song.
A path taken, yet unsure,
Longing for what felt secure.

In solitude we seek the truth,
Finding solace in our youth.
Twilight hangs, a fragile thread,
Binding dreams that lie ahead.

But as the sun begins to rise,
Strength is found in the goodbyes.
Independence calls us near,
With hopeful hearts, we conquer fear.

Two Voices, One Song

In harmony we find our way,
Two paths merge into the day.
Your laughter dances with my sighs,
We weave the moment, time flies.

Distinct yet bound, we share the beat,
Melodies through us softly meet.
Voices blend like colors bright,
Creating warmth within the night.

The verses rise and fall as one,
Underneath the setting sun.
Through trials faced, together strong,
In every note, we both belong.

A serenade made of our dreams,
In tangled paths, hope gently beams.
With every twist, we find our way,
Together facing a brand new day.

Two voices echo through the air,
Unison found in love and care.
And as we sing, let spirits soar,
For in our song, we are much more.

Navigating Uncertainty

In shadows deep, the road ahead,
Questions linger, hopes are fed.
With choices scattered like the leaves,
Each step forward, the heart believes.

The compass spins without a guide,
As waves of doubt crash like the tide.
Yet still we move, intent to find,
The hidden paths within the mind.

A flicker shines, a distant star,
Reminds us that we've come this far.
Through storms we brave, the unknown calls,
In every rise, a lesson falls.

Trust the flow, embrace the change,
Life's design might feel so strange.
In uncertainty, courage grows,
As new adventures start to show.

With each breath, we learn to steer,
To face the dark without the fear.
Navigating through the night,
Our hearts will guide us to the light.

Rhythms of Reciprocity

In tender moments, kindness blooms,
As laughter fills the empty rooms.
We give and take, a gentle dance,
Through fleeting glances, we take a chance.

The world spins round in borrowed time,
Each heartbeat drops a subtle rhyme.
With open hands, we share the load,
Creating joy on this shared road.

As daylight fades, we share our dreams,
In whispered thoughts, the heart redeems.
A cycle spins, a sacred thread,
Woven tales of tears we've shed.

Together bound by unseen strings,
In harmony, our spirit sings.
Through ups and downs, we find the way,
In giving love, we choose to stay.

The rhythms pulse in every deed,
In gratitude, we plant a seed.
For life's sweet symphony unfolds,
In reciprocity, our hearts are bold.

Co-authors of Destiny

In quiet corners, we weave our dreams,
Painting futures with vibrant seams.
Each word a brush, each thought a light,
Together we dance, in the deep of night.

Hand in hand, we chart the unknown,
In the realm of chances, seeds are sown.
With every step, our visions align,
Bound by purpose, your heart is mine.

Through valleys low, and mountains high,
We soar on wings, beneath the sky.
Our laughter echoes, a guiding song,
In this narrative, we both belong.

Time may test, but we stand firm,
Each twist in fate, a chance to learn.
With open hearts and voices strong,
In this journey, we all belong.

Together we write the tale of us,
In unity found, we place our trust.
Co-authors, partners, in life's grand play,
Crafting destiny, come what may.

Embrace of Allies

Through shadows cast, we find our way,
In the embrace of allies, we sway.
Lifting each other, in storms we stand,
Together weaving a single strand.

A bond unbroken, in trials we rise,
With whispered hopes and shared sunrise.
In laughter's warmth, our spirits soar,
Each heartbeat echoes, forevermore.

With open arms, we face the night,
Together shining, a radiant light.
In courage shared, we fight our fears,
The embrace of allies wipes away tears.

In the dance of life, no one alone,
In every challenge, our seeds are sown.
With steady hearts, we beat as one,
Through every battle, our strength is spun.

As anchors strong, we lift the weight,
In this journey shared, we celebrate.
From every moment, joy we pry,
In the embrace of allies, we fly.

Coalescence of Souls

In the stillness, our spirits blend,
Two hearts united, a timeless trend.
In whispered secrets, we find our depth,
A coalescence, a cosmic breadth.

Through the tapestry of life we weave,
In every rumor, in every leave.
With gentle grace, we forge our way,
A dance of souls, in night and day.

Together we rise, like morning dew,
In the essence of hope, forever true.
With every breath, our futures gleam,
Coalescing hearts, we share a dream.

Bound by purpose, unyielding thread,
In every moment, where love is spread.
With open arms, we greet the new,
In coalescence strong, we find our view.

As stars align our fates so bright,
In shared destiny, we ignite the night.
With courage infused, we face the toll,
In unity's grace, we become whole.

Navigating Together

Across the seas of chance we sail,
With guiding stars, and dreams to unveil.
In every ripple, our hopes arise,
Navigating together, beneath vast skies.

With maps of laughter, and winds of change,
We chart the course, through realms strange.
In distant lands, where shadows loom,
Our bond brings light, dispelling gloom.

Through tempest's roar, we hold our ground,
In courage found, our hearts resound.
No storm can sway this steadfast route,
Navigating together, we work it out.

With every step, we learn and grow,
In the rhythm of life, an endless flow.
In unity's strength, we find our way,
Navigating together, day by day.

With hands entwined, our spirits soar,
In the journey shared, we crave for more.
Together we write, through every endeavor,
As we navigate life, now and forever.

Shared Horizons

In the quiet dawn we meet,
Where shadows merge and retreat.
A whisper rides the gentle breeze,
Embracing hopes among the trees.

The sky unfurls its painted hue,
As dreams awaken, bold and new.
Together we walk this path of gold,
With stories waiting to be told.

We share the laughter, the tears that flow,
In harmony, our spirits grow.
What lies ahead is ours to chase,
In every moment, we find our place.

Through valleys deep and mountains high,
We chase the sun, we dare to fly.
With every step, our hearts align,
The world expands, our stars combine.

Beneath the vast and endless sky,
We walk as one, no need to try.
For in this union, we find our way,
Shared horizons guide our day.

Merging Destinies

Two rivers dance beneath the moon,
Their waters sing a timeless tune.
With currents strong and hearts entwined,
In this bond, our fates aligned.

Each twist and turn, a journey shared,
In every moment, we've both cared.
The world unfolds with every chance,
In destiny's vast, enduring dance.

Together we face the stormy night,
Holding on, we find the light.
Through trials faced and battles won,
Merging destinies, we become one.

As stars collide and spark a flame,
Our spirits whisper each other's name.
In the embrace of fate's design,
We wander forth, our dreams align.

With every heartbeat and shared sigh,
Through life's great tapestry, we fly.
So here's to paths forever weaved,
In merging destinies, we believe.

Convergence of Spirits

In the quiet moments, souls arise,
A convergence seen in the skies.
Two gentle hearts that face the dawn,
In unity, they blossom on.

With every glance, a spark ignites,
As shadows fade before the lights.
Each whispered word, a thread so fine,
Woven deep in love's design.

Through trials faced and laughter shared,
In every dream, we are prepared.
Our spirits dance like flames so bright,
In the embrace of endless night.

The world may shift like grains of sand,
But together, we take a stand.
In the silence, hear the tune,
A convergence beneath the moon.

As destinies intertwine with grace,
In every heartbeat, find your place.
With open hearts, we'll always thrive,
In this dance, we are alive.

Tandem Voyage

Across the waves, on seas so wide,
Together, we set forth with pride.
In every sunrise, new dreams awake,
A tandem voyage, we shall take.

With sails unfurled, we chase the breeze,
In harmony with the swaying trees.
Each whisper calls, a beacon bright,
Guiding our way through day and night.

From shores of hope to distant lands,
We journey forth, hand in hand.
Beyond the horizon, our spirits soar,
Tandem voyage, forevermore.

Through storms that rage and stars that shine,
In every moment, our hearts entwine.
No anchor holds us, we set the course,
Together forging an endless force.

With shared laughter and stories spun,
We sail the seas till day is done.
Bound by dreams that we explore,
In this tandem voyage, we ask for more.

Partnering Through Change

Together we stand, hand in hand,
Facing the currents, a shifting land.
With trust as our anchor, we start anew,
In storms of doubt, I lean on you.

Through trials we gather, our strength combined,
In laughter and tears, our hearts aligned.
In moments of silence, we find our way,
A dance of connection, come what may.

As seasons keep turning, we adapt and learn,
Embracing the lessons, for growth we yearn.
With courage ignited, we rise from the fall,
In the arms of each other, we can have it all.

Through valleys of shadows, we shine so bright,
Guiding each other from darkness to light.
With every step forward, our spirits entwined,
In the journey of change, true love we find.

So let us keep walking, through thick and thin,
In the heart of the storm, our love will begin.
Together, forever, with warmth in our gaze,
Partnering through change, we ignite the blaze.

Navigating the Unknown

A path uncharted, we take a chance,
With stars to guide us, we start our dance.
In the silence of night, fears take their flight,
Together we venture, igniting the light.

With every step taken, the future unfolds,
In whispers of courage, our story is told.
Hand in hand onward, through shadows we roam,
In the heart of the wild, we find our home.

The maps may be blank, but the journey is clear,
With dreams as our compass, we'll conquer our fear.
In moments uncertain, we seek and we find,
Strength in our bond, forever entwined.

Navigating the unknown, hearts beating as one,
Chasing horizons, our race has begun.
With faith in the journey, and hope as our guide,
The beauty of life we'll never let slide.

So here's to the risks, the joy, and the pain,
To the moments we'll gather, like sunshine after rain.
In life's great adventure, with you I'll stay,
Together we'll wander, come what may.

Secrets of Duet

In whispers of shadows, we share our song,
Harmonies weaving, where both hearts belong.
Two souls entwined, in a melody sweet,
A dance of emotions, a rhythmic heartbeat.

In the silence between notes, secrets reside,
In laughter and echoes, love won't subside.
Each lyric a story, each chorus a dream,
Together we flourish, a delicate theme.

As the world keeps spinning, we find our place,
In the art of connection, there's beauty and grace.
With every key played, a moment we capture,
In the secrets of duet, our hearts rapture.

The symphony swells, with each passing tide,
In the refuge of music, our feelings won't hide.
With passion ignited, we're fearless and bold,
In the warmth of our union, a tale to be told.

So let us keep singing, our hearts as the guide,
In the depths of the night, let our souls collide.
Two voices united, with love that won't fade,
In the secrets of duet, this magic we've made.

Threads of Resilience

In the fabric of life, we weave our dreams,
Stitching together, each thread brightly gleams.
Through trials we gather, in strength we grow,
With colors of courage, our spirits a glow.

As seasons keep changing, we stand up tall,
In the face of the storm, we will never fall.
With patience and grit, we weather each test,
In the tapestry of time, we find our rest.

Threads may get tangled, but we learn to mend,
In the hands of the heart, our journeys extend.
With laughter and love, we create and embrace,
Each moment a blessing, each challenge a grace.

Resilience is woven in the story we tell,
Through heartaches and joys, we rise and we swell.
In the loom of existence, together we stand,
With threads of connection, our futures are planned.

So let's cherish the fabric, the love that we spin,
In the moments of struggle, the strength lies within.
With threads of resilience, we embark on our quest,
In the pattern of life, we are truly blessed.

Fusion of Intentions

In the quiet of the night, we dream,
Hearts aligned, like a flowing stream.
Intentions blend, a vibrant hue,
Together, nothing we can't pursue.

Whispers carried by the wind,
Promises crafted, our souls pinned.
Fires ignited with every glance,
In this dance, we take a chance.

Paths entwined, no need for fear,
Every heartbeat, a note we hear.
Merging hopes in a sacred space,
An epic journey, we embrace.

Fading doubts like shadows retreat,
Woven stories, we feel complete.
With every step, our spirits soar,
Together, we are so much more.

In the tapestry of fate, we trust,
United visions, a bond robust.
In this fusion, love takes flight,
Guiding us through the starry night.

A Canvas of Conjoined Journeys

Upon the canvas, colors bleed,
Every stroke, a shared creed.
Journeys painted with bold designs,
In each corner, your hand aligns.

Footsteps echo on paths untold,
With every story, our hearts unfold.
Moments captured, rich and bright,
Together, we're a guiding light.

Every sunrise brings a hue,
Each dawn speaks of me and you.
In laughter's echo, joy resounds,
Love's artwork, where grace abounds.

As seasons shift and time flows fast,
Memories made are built to last.
In fields of dreams, we'll wander free,
A canvas drawn for you and me.

With every challenge, colors blend,
Our journeys loop and gently mend.
In the masterpiece of life we find,
The beauty of two souls combined.

We Write Together

In ink and paper, stories weave,
A narrative that we believe.
Words caress the page like rain,
Together, joy and sorrow's gain.

Chapter by chapter, hand in hand,
Writing tales that forever stand.
Every comma, a breath we share,
In every period, a moment rare.

As sentences flow, our hearts align,
In this tale, your soul meets mine.
With every plot twist, new horizons rise,
We craft our world under open skies.

Through the verses, we discover light,
In the silence, our dreams take flight.
With each stanza, we build our lore,
Together, forever, we will explore.

In the margins, our laughter shows,
In the dialogue, love overflows.
As we write, our hearts ignite,
A symphony of words, pure and bright.

Lifelines in Unison

In tangled roots, our lives connect,
Lifelines drawn with pure respect.
Through storms and suns, we navigate,
Together, we can elevate.

In the rhythm of the heart's refrain,
Harmony flows, easing the pain.
Like rivers merging into one,
In unity, our fears undone.

Every challenge, a chance to grow,
With open hearts, together we glow.
In the whispers of the evening breeze,
We find strength, our souls at ease.

Bound by threads of trust and care,
In shared moments, love's declare.
With hands entwined, we face the dawn,
In unison, we are reborn.

Through every trial, our spirits rise,
In every laugh, a sweet surprise.
Together we'll face the unknown path,
Lifelines entwined, igniting the math.

Collective Dreams

In the hush of night we gather,
Voices blend like flowing streams.
Whispers of hope weave a tapestry,
Together we nurture our dreams.

Under starlit skies we wander,
Chasing shadows, catching gleams.
Hearts united in the twilight,
Fueling the fire of our dreams.

Each story shared, a stepping stone,
Building bridges across our themes.
With every laugh and tear we find,
Strength in our collective dreams.

The world outside may seem distant,
But here our spirits burst at seams.
In a circle wrapped in magic,
We shine brighter in our dreams.

When dawn whispers its gentle greeting,
We rise, the sun's golden beams.
Hand in hand, we forge the future,
Together, it's more than just dreams.

The Light We Share

In the depths of darkest moments,
A flicker shines, our hearts align.
With every spark igniting softly,
We find warmth in the design.

Guided by the shared connection,
Though paths may twist and intertwine.
Together we reflect our essence,
A brilliance that's purely divine.

When shadows stretch across the landscape,
And doubt begins to cloud the mind,
Let's hold fast to one another,
In our hearts, the light we find.

In the chaos, we are steady,
Through the storms, our spirits shine.
With open hands and open hearts,
We nurture the light, so fine.

We sparkle in a world of wonder,
With love as our guiding sign.
In every glance, every gesture,
We illuminate the divine.

Ties That Bind

In silence shared, a bond is woven,
A tapestry of love and trust.
No distance can sever our connection,
In every heart, the ties are just.

Through trials faced and joys discovered,
We journey on, a steadfast crew.
With every memory, laughter echoes,
In the fabric of me and you.

Each moment lived becomes a thread,
Stitching pieces of our past.
Through joy and pain, we grow together,
This connection built to last.

When storms arise, we stand united,
Our spirits strong, our purpose clear.
With kindness, warmth and understanding,
We quiet every whispered fear.

Embracing differences, we flourish,
In harmony, we find our kind.
Through love and laughter, we discover
The beautiful ties that bind.

Rise Together

When darkness falls and hopes feel shattered,
We find strength in unity's glow.
With every step, we lift each other,
A chorus of voices, bold and slow.

The weight of the world feels lighter,
When many hearts beat as one.
In courage drawn from each other,
We welcome the rise of the sun.

Through the valleys low and mountains high,
With hands held firm, we will ascend.
The dreams we forge can't be broken,
With togetherness as our trend.

In the face of doubt, we gather,
Creating pathways we can see.
With every stride, we turn the tide,
Defying limits, wild and free.

Let's lift our eyes to brighter futures,
Emerging from shadows to soar.
In unity, we stand resilient,
Together, we rise evermore.

Unified by Purpose

In the light of shared dreams, we stand,
Bound by threads of hope, hand in hand.
Voices rise, a harmonious song,
Together we thrive, where we belong.

Through storms that shake, we hold tight,
Guided by stars, our hearts ignite.
Each step forward, our vision clear,
In unity's warmth, we cast out fear.

Dreams intertwine, under the same sky,
With every heartbeat, together we fly.
Purpose aligned, our spirits soar,
In the dance of life, we ask for more.

Branches may twist, but roots run deep,
In fields of trust, our harvest we reap.
Fueled by passion, our voices will blend,
Unified by purpose, our journey won't end.

The Cost of Togetherness

In laughter's echo, shadows creep,
Beneath the smiles, secrets we keep.
For every bond a price we pay,
In shared embrace, we lose our way.

Can hearts entwined find space to breathe?
In whispered words, there's much to leave.
Connections forged, yet burdens grow,
In the depths of closeness, pain can show.

Each sacrifice, a silent toll,
Navigating the depths of soul.
The joy we find may pierce like glass,
In wanting love, we let feelings pass.

Yet through the burdens, light can shine,
In shared moments, truth we define.
The cost is high, yet worth the fight,
Together we stand, in love's pure light.

Second Sight

In the hush of night, visions arise,
Whispers of truth dance in disguise.
A flicker of fate, the unseen lure,
In twilight's glow, the heart feels sure.

Glimpses of paths yet to unfold,
Stories of lives that cannot be told.
In the silence, clarity breaks,
Secrets of time, the soul awakes.

Eyes that see past the veils of time,
In shadows deep, the light will rhyme.
Moments to come, etched in the air,
With second sight, we move with care.

Steps of wisdom, bold and bright,
Guided by dreams that pulse with light.
In the realm where visions align,
We forge our fate, intertwine.

Every heartbeat, a thread of fate,
In dreams we're woven, it's never too late.
With second sight, we embrace the night,
Searching for truths, our spirits take flight.

Shelters of Solitude

In corners quiet, whispers rest,
Walls that cradle, feel like a nest.
Between the sighs, a space to breathe,
In solitude's arms, we find reprieve.

Amidst the clutter of life's loud rush,
A sanctuary made in the gentle hush.
Here in the stillness, voices grow faint,
In the heart's echo, we paint and we chant.

Time unfurls its delicate thread,
In layers of thought, our spirits are fed.
Each moment cherished, a treasure held tight,
Within the shadows, we seek the light.

With every heartbeat, quiet reveals,
The beauty found in what solitude heals.
In soft surrender, we learn to reflect,
Finding ourselves in what we protect.

In shelters of solitude, wisdom blooms,
In the sacred space, the heart resumes.
With open arms, we embrace the divine,
In quietude's blessings, our souls intertwine.

Companions on a Journey

Together we walk on winding roads,
With dreams in our hearts, and lightened loads.
Through forests deep and mountains high,
With every step, we learn to fly.

The sun may fade, and storms may rise,
Yet, hand in hand, we share the skies.
In laughter's echo, or silence' grace,
Each moment shared, a warm embrace.

We chase the dawn, we greet the night,
In every struggle, we find the light.
The paths may twist, the rocks may slide,
But with your strength, I will abide.

The journey shaped by tales we weave,
In every heartbeat, we believe.
Though miles may stretch and years may pass,
With you beside, I see each glass.

So, here we stand, where dreams unite,
Two souls together, fierce and bright.
In every chapter, love's refrain,
Companions on this endless train.

When Shadows Embrace

In the twilight when day departs,
The shadows dance, yet warm our hearts.
In whispered secrets, they softly creep,
Holding stories in the dark, they keep.

Beneath the moon, a silver glow,
The world transforms, a gentle flow.
In every corner, fears may hide,
Yet shadows cradle, our hopes inside.

With every flicker, they intertwine,
Creating patterns, both yours and mine.
A symphony of silence, vast,
When shadows embrace, sorrows are cast.

Each whispered breath, a moment shared,
In hushed reflections, souls laid bare.
Together we wander, lost yet found,
In shadow's grasp, true love is crowned.

So let us dance where shadows play,
In twilight's arms, we'll gently sway.
In every corner of this space,
Our souls entwined as shadows embrace.

A Tapestry of Two

In threads of laughter, woven tight,
A tapestry of joy ignites the night.
Each color vibrant, each texture rare,
A story shared, beyond compare.

In moments stitched with love and care,
We build a world that's rich and rare.
With golden hopes and silver dreams,
A tapestry of life, it gleams.

Through trials faced, through storms that blow,
Each knot reminds us we'll ever grow.
In fabric strong, our hearts align,
In every twist, your hand in mine.

As seasons shift and time unfolds,
Our tapestry tells of bravery bold.
With every thread, our tale takes flight,
A dance of shadows, a burst of light.

So let us weave, with colors true,
A tapestry crafted, me and you.
In every stitch, a promise new,
Together forever, a tapestry of two.

Unbreakable Chains

In laughter and tears, our bond is formed,
Through tempests and trials, we stay warm.
Each link a story, every moment shared,
In unbreakable chains, our souls are bared.

With steadfast love, we stand our ground,
In shadows deep, our light is found.
Through heavy storms and sudden rains,
Each heartbeat echoes, unbreakable chains.

In whispered hopes and dreams yet to see,
Together we thrive, you and me.
When fears arise, we break each pain,
With every bond forged, unbreakable chains.

In joy, we soar, in sorrow we kneel,
With every struggle, our strength is real.
The past may haunt, but love remains,
Interwoven steadfast, unbreakable chains.

So hand in hand, let's face the dawn,
In every challenge, love will spawn.
Through thick and thin, this truth sustains,
Forever bound by unbreakable chains.

Tandem Threads

In quiet spaces, two hearts weave,
A tapestry of dreams, we believe.
With every thread, a story spun,
Together as one, our journey begun.

In laughter shared, we find our song,
Through storms we face, we still belong.
Stitched with care, our paths align,
A bond of trust, in love we shine.

In whispers soft, our secrets flow,
A dance of shadows, light will glow.
With hands entwined, we face the night,
In tandem steps, we seek the light.

Through ups and downs, we stand tall,
In unity's grasp, we'll never fall.
Each moment cherished, a precious thread,
In the fabric of life, our hopes are fed.

In the quiet dawn, our dreams take flight,
Two souls united, hearts ignited.
Together we weave, through time and space,
In tandem threads, we find our grace.

A Symphony of Voices

In harmony's embrace, we rise and sing,
A chorus bright, the joy we bring.
Each voice a note, in tune with the rest,
Together we flourish, in unity blessed.

With whispers soft, or thunder loud,
We share our truths, and stand proud.
In every heart, a melody grows,
The beauty of voices, the world it shows.

Through rhythms shared, we dance as one,
Creating waves as bright as the sun.
Each note a promise, each pause a chance,
In this grand symphony, we find our dance.

From quiet moments, to joyous cries,
A tapestry woven, beneath vast skies.
In every heartbeat, every refrain,
A symphony of voices, a sweet gain.

Let the music guide, let the spirits soar,
In every echo, we seek for more.
Together in harmony, hand in hand,
A symphony of voices, forever we stand.

Bridges of Understanding

Across the waters, a bridge extends,
Built on respect, where kindness blends.
With every step, we learn and grow,
Building connections, letting love flow.

In shared stories, we find our place,
With open hearts, we embrace grace.
Each difference cherished, a lesson learned,
Through bridges of understanding, wisdom is earned.

In the silence held, or laughter shared,
We break down walls, showing we cared.
Through empathy's gaze, we see the whole,
Bridges we build, connect every soul.

In unity's strength, we find our way,
With every bridge, we seize the day.
Together we walk, in peace we stand,
Bridges of understanding, hand in hand.

The world may divide, but we unite,
With compassion's light, we shine bright.
From heart to heart, we send a spark,
Bridges of understanding, igniting the dark.

Duality in Motion

In the dance of shadows, light does play,
Two sides of life, in vivid display.
With every heartbeat, opposites meet,
In duality's rhythm, we find our beat.

The sun and moon take turns to reign,
In harmony's grasp, joy and pain.
Each moment fleeting, yet deeply known,
In duality's embrace, we find our home.

From laughter's peak to sorrow's depth,
In every breath, there's a story kept.
A tapestry woven, both dark and bright,
In the dance of duality, we find our light.

Through rise and fall, our spirits soar,
Balancing each other, forevermore.
In the beauty of both, we are set free,
Duality in motion, just you and me.

Through every tempest, we learn to stand,
Embracing both sides, hand in hand.
In life's rich dance, as time flows on,
Duality in motion, forever strong.

Collective Resilience

In the face of rising tides,
We stand together, side by side.
With every challenge, every test,
Our spirits soar, we give our best.

Roots intertwined beneath the ground,
In unity, our strength is found.
We lift each other when we fall,
Together we can conquer all.

Through stormy nights and blazing days,
We forge our path in countless ways.
In shared burdens, our hearts ignite,
And with our love, we light the night.

Every heartbeat, every sigh,
Forms the bond that won't run dry.
Like stars that shine in darkest skies,
Our hope will always rise and rise.

Collective spirit, fierce and bold,
A tale of courage to be told.
In harmony, we will prevail,
Our legacy; a timeless tale.

Dance of the Kindred

Beneath the moon, we gather close,
With gentle whispers, hearts engrossed.
A dance of souls, entwined in chance,
In the twilight, we find our dance.

Hands reach out, as laughter flows,
In every step, our spirit grows.
We twirl like leaves in autumn's breeze,
Our kinship sings with perfect ease.

With every spin, a story told,
Of dreams and hopes, of love and bold.
In unity, our shadows blend,
Together here, our hearts transcend.

The rhythm calls, our spirits soar,
As we embrace what lies in store.
Through every beat, our courage gleams,
We dance in sync with vibrant dreams.

And as the stars begin to wane,
We hold this night, joy without pain.
For in this dance, the world we mend,
A tapestry, where souls transcend.

Merging Shadows

In twilight's glow, our shadows meet,
Silhouettes where stillness greets.
With whispered secrets, we align,
A dance of spirits, pure and fine.

As dusk descends, our stories blend,
In the dark, the light can mend.
Each heartbeat echoes, soft and low,
In this embrace, our truths will flow.

A canvas painted in muted tones,
Where hidden whispers find their homes.
We walk together, side by side,
Through fading light, our hearts collide.

Entwined in shadow, we unite,
Facing fears that haunt the night.
From silence blooms, a song so sweet,
Within these shadows, hope's heartbeat.

Tomorrow's dawn will break anew,
But in this moment, we pursue.
The merging of our souls, a grace,
In shadows deep, we find our place.

The Strength of Many

A chorus rising, voices strong,
Through trials faced, we will belong.
Each hand extended, bonds we weave,
In unity, we choose to believe.

Like rivers flowing into one,
Together, we can overcome.
With every heartbeat, every cheer,
The strength of many draws us near.

Mountains tall will shake and sway,
When all our hopes light up the way.
In every struggle, find the grace,
A tapestry that time won't erase.

We lift each other through the strife,
Each story told, a precious life.
In unity, we'll rise above,
Bound by the thread of endless love.

In our resolve, a fire burns,
With every lesson, life we learn.
Together, we can change the day,
The strength of many leads the way.

The Fragrance of Friendship

In the garden where laughter blooms,
Scented whispers fill the rooms.
Colors bright and spirits high,
True friends dance beneath the sky.

In every smile a memory made,
In every hug a bond displayed.
Through seasons change, we stand so tall,
In unity, we'll conquer all.

The fragrance lingers, soft and sweet,
A cherished joy, a heart's heartbeat.
Companions dear, forever near,
In this embrace, we lose our fear.

With open hearts, we share our dreams,
In every challenge, trust redeems.
Together we rise, together we fall,
In friendship's light, we have it all.

So here's to us, in laughter and tears,
A bond that grows throughout the years.
Through every storm, through every strife,
The fragrance of friendship breathes new life.

A Blueprint for Us

On the canvas of dreams, we lay our plans,
Guided by purpose, with strong, steady hands.
Every stroke crafted with care and thought,
A masterpiece waiting, so deeply sought.

In the blueprint we sketch, our hopes intertwine,
Foundations of trust, designed to align.
Brick by brick, we build our way,
Through sunlit skies and clouds of gray.

With laughter and love, we pave our path,
Drawing maps of joy, avoiding wrath.
Together we'll draft a future so bright,
A vision of us, chasing the light.

Each moment a tile, each memory a door,
As we shape our world, we rediscover more.
In unity's grasp, we create our space,
A blueprint for us, a bond we embrace.

So let us design, with every heartbeat,
A journey together, both tender and sweet.
In the heart of our dream, we flourish and trust,
Forever defining our blueprint of us.

Holding the Flame Alight

In the stillness of night, a flicker appears,
A spark of connection that conquers our fears.
With gentle hands, we nurture the glow,
Holding the flame through high winds that blow.

Together we stand, united in light,
Illuminating paths that can lead us from fright.
Through trials and storms, we'll never let go,
As long as our love continues to grow.

With whispered words, we feed the fire,
Stoking the warmth of our shared desire.
Each moment a gift, so precious and rare,
In holding this flame, we banish despair.

The flames may flicker, but never will fade,
In this sacred bond, our dreams are laid.
And though shadows loom, we'll always ignite,
Together we're stronger, holding the flame alight.

So let the world turn, and the wild winds weave,
For in love's embrace, we choose to believe.
With passion and hope, we soar to new heights,
Forever together, holding the flame alight.

Pulses in Sync

Two hearts beat in rhythm, a dance divine,
With every pulse, our souls intertwine.
In the silence between, a melody's beat,
Unfolding a story, so vivid, so sweet.

In the glow of the moment, time slows its pace,
As emotions flow, we find our place.
In laughter and tears, our pulses align,
A symphony crafted, both yours and mine.

With every heartbeat, a promise we share,
In the fabric of life, we thread with care.
Entwined like the vines, our love will grow,
A garden of dreams, in sunlight's soft glow.

Through valleys of shadows, through mountains so high,
With synchronized beats, we reach for the sky.
In the tapestry woven, our spirits infuse,
Pulses in sync, it's love that we choose.

So here's to the journey, the rhythm we find,
In the pulse of our hearts, our paths intertwined.
Forever we'll dance, in this delicate sway,
Pulses in sync, come what may.

Convergence of Hearts

Two souls wandering, lost in the night,
They found each other, a spark ignites.
Whispers of love in the shadows blend,
A beautiful journey, a heart on the mend.

Hands intertwined, as fate calls their name,
In stillness they rise, none feeling the same.
Hopeful horizons that stretch far and wide,
Together they'll conquer, side by side.

Through stormy weather, their bond stays strong,
In laughter and tears, where they both belong.
With every heartbeat, a rhythm divine,
A promise forever, their hearts intertwine.

As day turns to night, and seasons will change,
They nurture their love, it feels so strange.
In the light of the moon, secrets unfold,
A tale of two heartbeats, forever retold.

At the end of the road, where dreams shall unite,
They'll hold onto love, through dark and through light.
With every adventure, new paths they will chart,
In the convergence of souls, they'll never depart.

Conjoined Aspirations

Two dreams raised high on a shared golden thread,
They rise like the sun, forging paths, they tread.
In unity, visions take flight and expand,
Together they build, with a steadfast hand.

Mountains may echo with doubts that arise,
But courage will shine behind hopeful eyes.
With every heartbeat, their spirits ignite,
Chasing horizons, they reach for the light.

The world is a canvas, they color with care,
As laughter and dreams weave the fruits that they share.
In gardens of joy, their aspirations bloom,
Conjoined in their quest, dispelling all gloom.

Through trials and triumphs, they lift each other,
With love as their compass, one sister, one brother.
Each step brings them nearer to what they both seek,
In the rhythm of life, united and sleek.

Celebrating small wins, they dance through the night,
Two souls moving forward, a beautiful sight.
Their dreams intertwine, as they find their own way,
In the tapestry woven, together they stay.

The Force of Togetherness

In gentle embrace, they gather their might,
Facing the world with hearts burning bright.
With laughter like music, their spirits arise,
A force of connection under wide-open skies.

Through valleys of shadows and mountains of light,
They stand as a beacon, their bond feels so right.
In moments of silence, the strength they do gain,
Together, forever, they'll weather the pain.

Their dreams intertwine like branches of trees,
While whispers of hope dance on each soft breeze.
The warmth of their love is a radiant fire,
A force of togetherness every heart can inspire.

When storms make them tremble, they're anchored in trust,
In laughter and sorrow, they flourish and rust.
Hand in hand walking, through thick and through thin,
The journey is sweeter when two are akin.

As dawn greets the night, they share in the glow,
Planting seeds of their story, together they'll grow.
In unity's spell, they tap into fate,
The force of togetherness, love's everlasting state.

Synergy of Spirits

In twilight's embrace, where dreams intertwine,
Two spirits converge, a dance so divine.
With laughter like starlight, they spark in the gloam,
Creating a haven, a place they call home.

Moments of silence, like whispers, they share,
In corridors echoing love's gentle care.
Through trials and triumphs, they're stronger in bond,
In synergy's glow, they endlessly respond.

They weave through the streets, hand in hand, side by side,
Creating a tapestry, joy is their guide.
Facing the world with hearts intertwined,
The synergy of spirits, beautifully aligned.

With every adventure, they cultivate grace,
In the warmth of their presence, they find their own place.

A fortress of love, they build day by day,
In the synergy of spirits, forever they'll stay.

As seasons may change and years slip away,
Their bond will endure, come what may.
With dreams as their compass, they gracefully soar,
Together in harmony, forever more.

Hand in Hand

Through the fields we wander wide,
With laughter echoing inside.
Every step a gentle trace,
Together we embrace this space.

The sun sets low, a golden hue,
In your eyes, the world feels new.
Hand in hand, we forge ahead,
With love that's pure, with dreams widespread.

When shadows creep and doubts arise,
I find my strength within your eyes.
With every heartbeat, we will stand,
Together strong, we're always planned.

In storms we face, through rain and snow,
Our bond will only ever grow.
With faith that cannot break or bend,
We journey far, together, friend.

At twilight's call, we pause to see,
The beauty found in you and me.
With whispers soft of hopes and dreams,
Hand in hand, we craft our themes.

A Symphony of Kindred

In harmony we sing our song,
With notes that flow both bright and strong.
Each voice a thread, a vibrant hue,
Together woven, pure and true.

The rhythms dance beneath the stars,
Casting aside both doubts and scars.
With every beat, our hearts align,
A melody that's yours and mine.

Through quiet moments, we create,
A symphony that won't abate.
The laughter shared, the tears that fall,
In every note, we hear the call.

From mountains high to valleys low,
Our music flows, a gentle glow.
In time's embrace, we shall ascend,
This vibrant song, it has no end.

As seasons change and stories blend,
Our harmony will never end.
In every heartbeat, we shall find,
A symphony of heart and mind.

Uniting for Tomorrow

With hopeful eyes, we gaze ahead,
In dreams of peace, our spirits fed.
A world transformed, we dare to see,
With hearts aligned, united, free.

Through open hands and shared embrace,
We cultivate a sacred space.
Each step we take, a seed we plant,
For love and kindness, we give chant.

In every challenge we shall rise,
With strength and courage, reach the skies.
For every voice that dares to speak,
Shall pave the path for those who seek.

Together now, we carve the way,
In unity, we'll seize the day.
The light of hope, it brightly shines,
As love's great tide, forever binds.

In every heartbeat, every smile,
We walk together, mile by mile.
With open hearts, our dreams we'll claim,
Uniting for tomorrow's flame.

Reflections in Each Other

In quiet moments, we shall find,
Reflections deep and intertwined.
With whispered thoughts and knowing glances,
We dance through life's many chances.

In laughter shared, in tears we shed,
We mirror truths, where love has led.
Each story told, a shared refrain,
Together woven through joy and pain.

As seasons change, and faces age,
We turn the leaf, we write the page.
Through every challenge, side by side,
In mutual strength, we will abide.

When shadows fall and fears arise,
Our hearts will shine, we'll take the skies.
For in your eyes, I see the light,
Reflections of our shared delight.

In every moment we embrace,
The tender warmth of our own grace.
Together, dear, we find our flow,
Reflections in each other grow.

Harmony in Unity

In twilight's embrace, we gather here,
Voices blend softly, calming each fear.
Hands intertwined, a circle we've made,
In this gentle warmth, our hearts are laid.

Through storms and trials, we stand as one,
With every step taken, new journeys begun.
Together we rise, like the morning sun,
A melody sweet, in harmony spun.

With laughter and joy, our spirits ignite,
In the dance of life, we shine so bright.
United we sing, through day and through night,
In the heart of community, we find our light.

In silence we listen, to stories unfold,
The wisdom of ages, in whispers retold.
Nurtured by kindness, our futures be bold,
In the tapestry woven, our love we uphold.

Together we'll flourish, through challenges faced,
With faith as our anchor, we'll never be displaced.
Embracing the journey, with hope interlaced,
For in unity's heart, our dreams are embraced.

Bonds of Tomorrow

Seeds of tomorrow, we plant with care,
In fields of friendship, we sow love rare.
With trust as our soil, and dreams as the sun,
Together we thrive, our hearts gently spun.

Every moment cherished, each laughter we share,
In shadows we find, a strength that we bear.
Through the highs and lows, we stand hand in hand,
Our journeys entwined, like tides on the sand.

In the dance of our lives, each step is unique,
Yet the rhythm of hope is what we seek.
For bonds of tomorrow, we nurture with grace,
In the harmony woven, we find our place.

With every heartbeat, new dreams we create,
In the light of our bond, we illuminate fate.
Sharing our visions, we boldly aspire,
Together we climb, reaching ever higher.

Some days may be stormy, and skies may turn gray,
But together we'll shine, chasing clouds far away.
In the warmth of our love, we'll weather each gale,
Through every adventure, together we'll sail.

Together We Flourish

In gardens of kindness, we plant our dreams,
Through laughter and joy, we nurture our seams.
Each moment a petal, unfolding so rare,
Together we flourish, our spirits laid bare.

With hearts full of courage, we step into light,
Facing every challenge, embracing the bright.
In the whispers of nature, our souls intertwine,
Creating a future where hope brightly shines.

Through seasons of change, we grow side by side,
In the dance of our lives, there's nothing to hide.
Together we venture, through valleys and peaks,
In unity's embrace, it's connection we seek.

The laughter we share, like a soft summer breeze,
Bringing warmth to our hearts, putting minds at ease.
Every thread of our story, together we weave,
A tapestry vibrant, in love we believe.

In the warmth of our bond, we find there is power,
With each day unfolding, like petals of flower.
Our spirits together, so strong and so free,
In this journey of growth, it's you and it's me.

Allies in Echoes

In the silence that lingers, we hear our hearts call,
Fragmented and whole, we rise from the fall.
Allies in echoes, we share in the sound,
With complexities woven, our souls are unbound.

Together, we wander through shadows and light,
Finding strength in the struggle, igniting the night.
In laughter and tears, our stories are clear,
As allies in echoes, we conquer our fear.

When storms try to pull us, we anchor our dreams,
In the chorus of friendship, we thrive in our streams.
Every voice a reminder, we're never alone,
Together we flourish, in love we have grown.

In moments of doubt, when the path seems unclear,
We stand close together, erasing the fear.
With hearts intertwined, we're a beacon of hope,
As allies in echoes, we learn how to cope.

Across every distance, our spirits remain,
With whispers of kindness, we soften the pain.
In the tapestry woven, our hearts beat as one,
Together we shine, till the race is all run.

The Strength of Us

In unity we stand, hand in hand,
Facing storms, we find our land.
With hearts ablaze, we share the light,
Together, we'll conquer the night.

Through trials faced, we grow more bold,
Our bond, a story waiting to be told.
With whispers of hope, we rise again,
In this dance of life, we feel no pain.

Strength in numbers, a force unbroken,
In silent vows, our promise spoken.
For every tear, we'll dry with grace,
In every challenge, find our place.

With laughter woven in every thread,
Our spirits soar, no longer misled.
Together we stand, fierce as the sun,
In this journey of life, we are one.

So let us roam, with courage high,
Embracing love as our ally.
For in this life, we shall endure,
The strength of us, forever pure.

Together Against the Tide

When waves crash down, we hold our ground,
In the deepest sea, our strength is found.
With every heartbeat, we swim as one,
Together, we'll rise with the morning sun.

The currents pull, but our will is strong,
In the darkest hours, we sing our song.
With hands entwined, we face the strife,
Together against the tides of life.

With courage fierce and spirits bright,
We navigate the stormy night.
Through the tempests, we'll find our way,
Together we fight, come what may.

In the shifting sands of time and fate,
Our bond unites, we navigate.
For every obstacle, we'll strive to find,
A path together, our hearts aligned.

So side by side, let us endure,
With every challenge, we will mature.
Together we'll weather the fiercest tide,
In this dance of life, we won't divide.

Serendipitous Connections

In the quiet moments, chance does play,
We find each other in a wondrous way.
Two souls collide in the fabric of time,
Creating harmony, a silent rhyme.

With smiles exchanged on a bustling street,
Life's beautiful rhythm, a gentle beat.
In laughter shared, we break the ice,
These fleeting moments, oh, how nice!

From unexpected places, bonds will grow,
In hearts entwined, our spirits glow.
Through serendipity, we learn to trust,
In honest connections, we find our must.

With every meeting, a story unfolds,
In whispered secrets, our truth is told.
Each moment cherished, a precious find,
In this dance of life, we're intertwined.

So here's to the magic that life can bestow,
In the serendipity of friends we know.
For every heart that we meet and blend,
Is a beautiful spark, a lifelong friend.

Informed by Empathy

In the tapestry of life, threads intertwined,
Empathy blooms where hearts are aligned.
With open ears and mindful sight,
We bridge the gaps that dim our light.

With every story that we embrace,
We cultivate kindness, a warm space.
In the silence of understanding, we grow,
Informed by empathy, our spirits flow.

Through struggles shared and burdens eased,
A world united, our hearts felled please.
With compassion's touch, we heal the divide,
In the call of each other, we take pride.

For every tear, there's a story untold,
In every challenge, there's courage unfold.
Together we'll rise, with hearts so free,
Informed by empathy, we will see.

So let us walk with kindness in tow,
With empathy's light, we'll ever glow.
In the journey of life, hand in hand,
With empathy guiding, together we stand.

Milton Keynes UK
Ingram Content Group UK Ltd.
UKHW021208261024
450281UK00007B/110